Pet Care

Kittens

Niki Walker & Bobbie Kalman

Photographs by Marc Crabtree

Crabtree Publishing Company

www.crabtreebooks.com

Kittens

A Bobbie Kalman Book

Dedicated by Marc Crabtree
To Natalie and Niki Noseworthy—two great animal lovers!

Editor-in-Chief
Bobbie Kalman

Writing team
Niki Walker
Bobbie Kalman

Substantive editor
Kathryn Smithyman

Project editor
Rebecca Sjonger

Editors
Molly Aloian
Amanda Bishop
Kelley MacAulay

Art director
Robert MacGregor

Design
Margaret Amy Reiach

Production coordinator
Heather Fitzpatrick

Photo research
Crystal Foxton

Consultant
Dr. Michael A. Dutton, DVM, DABVP, Weare Animal Hospital,
www.weareanimalhospital.com

Special thanks to
Jeremy Payne, Dave Payne, Shelbi Setikas, Bailee Setikas,
Arunas Setikas, Sheri Setikas, Gloria Nesbitt, Lateesha Warner,
Connie Warner, Kathy Middleton, Jenn Randall and Bonsai,
Vanessa Diodatti, Mike Cipryk and PETLAND

Photographs
John Daniels/ardea.com: page 8
© CORBIS/MAGMA: page 14 (top)
Marc Crabtree: front cover, pages 3, 5 (top), 12, 13, 14 (bottom),
    15, 16, 17 (top and bottom), 18, 19, 20, 21, 22, 23, 24, 25,
    29, 30, 31
Siede Preis/Getty Images: page 6
© Superstock: pages 9 (middle), 26
Other images by PhotoDisc, Digital Stock, and Comstock

Illustrations
Margaret Amy Reiach: pages 17, 27

Digital prepress
Embassy Graphics

Printer
Worzalla Publishing Company

Crabtree Publishing Company
www.crabtreebooks.com   1-800-387-7650

PMB 16A
350 Fifth Avenue
Suite 3308
New York, NY
10118

612 Welland Avenue
St. Catharines
Ontario
Canada
L2M 5V6

73 Lime Walk
Headington
Oxford
OX3 7AD
United Kingdom

Cataloging-in-Publication Data
Walker, Niki.
  Kittens / Niki Walker & Bobbie Kalman;
photographs by Marc Crabtree.
    p. cm. -- (Pet care series)
  Includes index.
  ISBN 0-7787-1750-X (RLB) -- ISBN 0-7787-1782-8 (pbk.)
  1. Kittens--Juvenile literature. 2. Cats--Juvenile literature.
[1. Cats. 2. Animals--Infancy. 3. Pets.] I. Kalman, Bobbie.
II. Crabtree, Marc ill. III. Title. IV. Series.
SF445.7.W36 2004
636.8'07--dc22

2003024979
LC

Contents

What are kittens?

Kittens are young cats. Cats are **mammals**.
Mammals are animals that have backbones.
They have hair or fur on their bodies. A baby
mammal drinks milk from its mother's body.

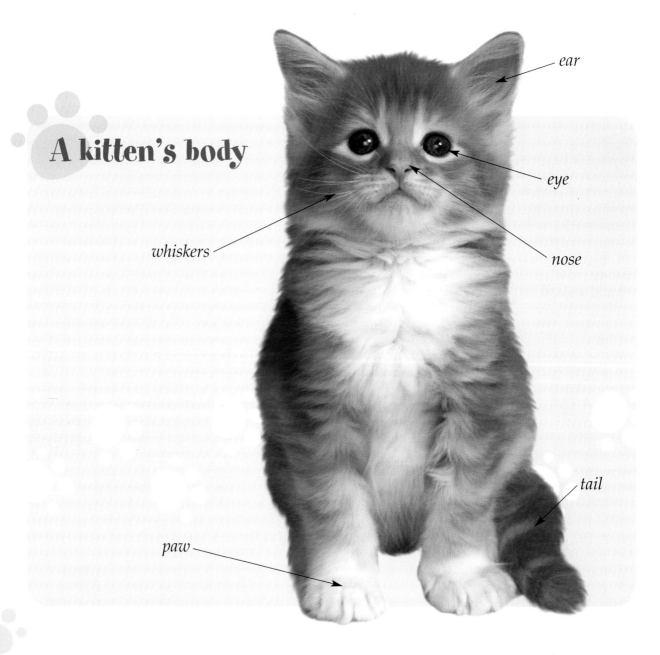

A kitten's body

ear

eye

nose

whiskers

tail

paw

Wild cats

Pet cats are related to lions, tigers, leopards, and other **wild cats**. Wild cats chase and eat other animals for food. They do not live with people. Pet cats are similar to wild cats, but they are not wild. Pet cats live with their owners, who feed them and care for them with a lot of love!

Like wild cats, pet cats are good at jumping, climbing, and running.

The right pet for you?

Cats are smart, cute, and loving. They enjoy playing with people and can be very frisky! Cats are also happy being on their own. They are good pets for people who are away from home during the day.

Kitten care

Kittens depend on people for food and water. They also need love and attention. You will need an adult's help to care for your kitten or cat.

Would you be a good kitten owner?

Are you ready?

The questions below will help you and your family decide if you are ready for a kitten.

- Will you clean up after your kitten every day?

- Can you spend a half hour every day playing with a kitten?

- Most cats live from twelve to twenty years. Will you take care of your cat for many years to come?

- Is anyone in your family **allergic** to cats?

- Do you know how much it costs to care for a cat? A cat can cost a family around $350 a year. It may cost more if the cat needs special care.

So many cats!

There are about 100 **breeds**, or kinds, of pet cats. The cats in each breed look similar and have the same **traits**. Some breeds are more friendly or playful than others. A **purebred** cat has parents and grandparents that are the same breed. Purebreds can be expensive. A few of the most popular breeds are shown on these pages.

Persian cats have long fur, small ears, and flat faces. They are very friendly cats.

Siamese cats are very smart.
They are long and thin
with large, pointy ears.

Maine Coon cats are a large,
strong breed. They are playful,
even as they grow older.

All mixed up!

Many pet cats are **mixed breeds**. A mixed-
breed cat has relatives that are different
breeds. Mixed-breed cats are just as friendly
as purebred cats are. Some are even
healthier than purebreds.

Choosing your kitten

There are many places to get a kitten. You may find one at a local **animal shelter**. You can also buy a kitten from a pet store or a **breeder**. Before you do, make sure the store or breeder takes good care of animals.

Ask your friends and family if they know of anyone who is giving away kittens for free.

What to look for

Take your time when you are choosing your kitten. Ask to hold it. Does it seem to like you? Make sure it is healthy and friendly. Look for:

- soft, smooth fur

- clean ears

- bright, clear eyes with no **crust** in the corners

- a soft, damp nose that feels cool and does not run or have a crust

- a pink mouth and gums

- a clean bottom

- curious, playful, and friendly behavior

Getting ready

Before you bring your new pet home, you need to get ready. There are some things you can buy that will make it easier to take care of your kitten. These pages show what you will need.

*Your kitten should travel from place to place in a **carrier**.*

*Set up a **litter box** with clean litter in it.*

Some litter boxes come with covers.

*Your kitten should always wear a **collar** with a tag that has your phone number on it.*

bristle brush

wire brush

You will need a brush to keep your kitten looking and feeling good.

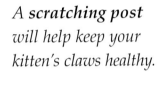

*A **scratching post** will help keep your kitten's claws healthy.*

Your kitten needs its own bowls for food and water.

Your kitten may like its own soft, snug bed.

Welcome home!

Baby kittens are tiny and helpless. They must stay with their mothers until they are eight weeks old. Do not take a kitten home before it is old enough to leave its mother. If you do, the kitten may not grow up properly.

A mother cat feeds her kittens milk from her body.

Hide-and-seek

Your kitten may hide when you bring it home. Do not pull your kitten from its hiding place. Let it come out when it feels ready.

A special time

The first few weeks with your kitten are important. If you treat your kitten well, it will learn to love and trust you. Let your kitten sleep when it is tired.

Handle with care

Always be gentle with your pet! Use two hands to lift your kitten. Place one hand under its front legs and the other hand under its bottom. Now, gently lift the kitten. If it tries to squirm away, set it down softly.

Be careful not to squeeze your kitten!

Meow chow

Kittens need certain foods to stay healthy. Most packaged foods have just the right **nutrients** for cats. Cats of different ages need different nutrients. Buy food that is made for your kitten or cat.

What's for dinner?

If you know which type of food your kitten ate before it came to live with you, do not change it. Try to stick with one brand of food. The label will tell you how much to give your pet each day.

Dry food is good for your cat's teeth. It can sit in a bowl all day.

Do not leave **canned food** out in a dish for more than an hour.

Semi-moist food may be less healthy than canned or dry food.

Not on the menu!

Be very careful not to give your kitten any food that will make it sick!

- Never feed dog food to your kitten.

- Give your kitten bits of cooked meat only as a treat. Do not give it bones!

- Eating **dairy foods** such as milk or ice cream can upset your kitten's stomach.

- Never feed your pet raw meat or eggs!

- Chocolate will make your kitten sick.

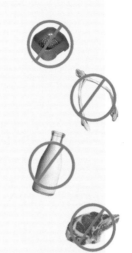

Food and fresh water

Kittens need to be fed four times a day. Adult cats should be fed twice a day. Your pet must always have fresh water in its bowl. Rinse and refill the bowl at least twice a day.

Try to feed your kitten at the same times every day.

The litter box

Teaching your kitten to use a litter box is not difficult. If its mother used a litter box, your kitten may already know how to use one.

Litter tips

Here are a few tips that will help your kitten learn how to use the litter box.

- Use the same type of litter your kitten used before you brought it home.

- After your kitten eats, always put it into the litter box.

- If your kitten has an accident, do not punish it. Gently place your kitten in its litter box to teach it where to go next time.

Be patient while your kitten is learning to use its litter box.

Keep it clean

Your kitten depends on you to keep its litter box clean. If you do not, your pet may get sick. It may also decide to use another part of your house as its bathroom!

Use the scoop!

Scoop out your kitten's waste every day. Once a week, dump all the litter into the trash. Scrub the litter box with hot, soapy water. Dry the box and refill it with clean litter. Always wash your hands well after scooping out and cleaning your kitten's litter box!

Ask an adult to help you pour the litter if the jug or bag is very heavy.

Pretty kitty

Your kitten will spend a lot of time cleaning itself. It licks its fur, chews its claws, and rubs its paws over its face. Your pet still needs your help to stay clean, though. **Grooming**, or cleaning, your kitten helps keep it healthy. It also helps you feel close to your pet.

Good grooming

Regular brushing will keep your kitten's fur soft and shiny.

- Gently rub the brush along your kitten's body. Smooth down its fur from head to tail.

- If your kitten has long fur, brush it with a wire brush every day. If your kitten has short fur, brush it with a bristle brush once a week.

- Check your kitten's skin as you groom it. Look for scrapes, cuts, and **fleas**.

More grooming tips

- If your kitten's ears, nose, or eyes are dirty, gently wipe them with a cotton ball dipped in warm water.

- Never cut your kitten's whiskers! It needs them to feel its way around.

- Ask your **veterinarian** to show you and your family how to trim your kitten's claws properly.

A veterinarian or "vet" is a medical doctor who treats animals. He or she helps you keep your pet healthy.

Clean teeth

Brush your kitten's teeth with a special toothbrush and toothpaste three times weekly. You may also give it teeth-cleaning treats. They will scrape your kitten's teeth clean as it chews on them.

Training tips

You can **train**, or teach, your kitten how to behave. You can also teach your kitten that some actions are not allowed, such as jumping on counters, scratching furniture, and biting fingers and toes. The younger your kitten is, the easier it is to train.

Good kitty, bad kitty

The way you behave will help your kitten learn what you want it to do.

- Always praise your kitten and reward it when it does something right.

- Never hit or yell at your kitten! Hitting and yelling will teach it to be afraid of you.

- Hiss, speak sternly, or squirt a little water from a spray bottle at your pet when it does something wrong.

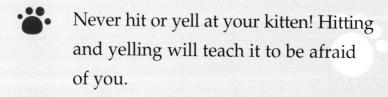

Here kitty, kitty!

One of the easiest things to teach your kitten is to come when you call it. Follow the steps shown on this page and be patient. You can follow these steps to teach your cat other things, too.

Hold out a treat for your kitten and call it by its name.

When your kitten comes to check out the treat, praise it and give it the treat right away.

Keep trying

Repeat this activity two or three times every day. Soon, your kitten will come every time it hears its name. Pet your kitten and praise it when it comes.

Play time

Kittens love to play! Cats are less frisky than kittens are, but they still need a lot of activity. Play time is especially important for indoor cats. Playing gives your cat exercise. Your kitten needs exercise to stay healthy. Spend at least a half hour every day playing with your cat or kitten. These pages show some popular—and safe—toys that your pet will love.

Toys on springs will bounce around in front of your kitten!

Toys and treats

Choose cat toys that are safe and fun. Try different types of toys until your kitten finds a favorite. It may also like **catnip** or cat grass. These plants will make it feel happy and excited.

Your kitten may like a toy mouse or a ball with a bell in it.

Understanding your kitten

Every kitten has its own way of **communicating**, or sending messages to people and other animals. Kittens make sounds such as meows and hisses. They also use **body language** to show what they are feeling.

Meow!

Cats meow for many reasons. They meow loudly when they feel insecure. Your kitten may also meow when it is hungry or wants your attention. You will soon know each meow that your pet makes.

Body language

To find out how your kitten is feeling, watch its fur, tail, and ears. If your cat is happy, its fur is smooth, its tail is raised, and its ears are pointed forward. If it is scared, its fur is standing up, its tail is lowered, and its ears are flat against its head. An angry cat may puff up its fur, swish its tail back and forth, and point its ears backward.

A happy cat points its ears forward and holds its tail high in the air.

An angry cat makes its fur stand on end so its body will look bigger to other animals.

A cat that is very scared will crouch down with its ears and tail flat against its body.

Safe kittens

Cats are a lot safer if they live indoors. They do not get in fights with other cats or catch illnesses. They do not get lost, stuck in trees, or hit by cars.

Indoor dangers

Indoor cats can face some dangers, however. They can become fat because they are less active, or eat things in your house that can hurt them. For example, your cat may become very ill if it eats some of your houseplants.

Indoor cats often live over ten years longer than do outdoor cats.

Outdoor cats

Outdoor cats get a lot of exercise, which may keep them healthy. Many outdoor cats catch diseases from other animals, though. Part of your job as a cat owner is to keep your pet safe. You must decide whether or not you think it is safe to let your kitten go outside. Never leave it outdoors overnight!

*Walk your kitten on a **leash** to keep it safe outdoors.*

Safety questions

Keep your kitten indoors if you answer "yes" to any of these questions:

- Is the weather where you live very cold and wet?

- Is there a busy road with a lot of traffic nearby?

- Are there dogs and cats or wild animals roaming around your neighborhood?

- Are there a lot of birds and nests in the area around your home?

Visiting a vet

Your kitten needs its first vet visit when it is about twelve weeks old. It must get **vaccinations** with needles. Vaccinations protect your pet from diseases. Your vet will tell you when you need to take your kitten to its next visit. It is also a good idea to ask the vet to **neuter** your kitten. A neutered cat cannot make kittens.

Yearly check-up

An adult cat needs a check-up once a year. The vet checks your cat's teeth, heart, and other body parts. Your cat may need shots every year to stay healthy.

Staying healthy

If your kitten is sick or injured, take it to the vet. Give your cat only the medicine your vet orders. Never give your cat medicine that is meant for people or other animals! If your pet is healthy, it will have a long life with you.

Hairballs

Your cat may swallow hairs when it licks its fur. Do not worry if your cat vomits up a **hairball**, or a lump of hair. Many cats vomit hairballs. Prevent hairballs by brushing and grooming your cat regularly.

When to get help

You know how your kitten normally looks and behaves. Your pet may be sick if it:

- sleeps more than usual

- drinks more water

- eats little or no food

- has a runny nose, dull or runny eyes, or dull-looking fur

- coughs, sneezes, or vomits a lot

Words to know

Note: Boldfaced words that are defined in the book may not appear on this page.

allergic Describing someone who has a physical reaction to something such as a food or animal dander

animal shelter A center that cares for animals that do not have homes

body language A type of communication that shows feelings by moving various body parts

breeder A person who brings cats together so the cats can make kittens

catnip A herb that makes cats excited when they eat it

crust Dried fluid that collects near a sick cat's eyes or nose

dairy foods Foods made with milk and milk products

fleas Tiny biting insects that live on the skin of animals

neuter To make an animal unable to make babies

nutrients Materials needed by a body to grow and stay healthy

trait A special characteristic, such as long fur or intelligence

vaccination A fluid that protects a body against diseases

veterinarian A medical doctor who treats animals

Index

1 2 3 4 5 6 7 8 9 0   Printed in the U.S.A.   3 2 1 0 9 8 7 6 5 4